IN A GRAIN OF SAND

IN A GRAIN OF SAND
Exploring Design by Nature

Andreas Feininger

Sierra Club Books
San Francisco

The Sierra Club, founded in 1892 by John Muir, has devoted itself to the study and protection of the earth's scenic and ecological resources—mountains, wetlands, woodlands, wild shores and rivers, deserts and plains. The publishing program of the Sierra Club offers books to the public as a nonprofit educational service in the hope that they may enlarge the public's understanding of the Club's basic concerns. The point of view expressed in each book, however, does not necessarily represent that of the Club. The Sierra Club has some sixty chapters coast to coast, in Canada, Hawaii, and Alaska. For information about how you may participate in its programs to preserve wilderness and the quality of life, please address inquiries to Sierra Club, 730 Polk Street, San Francisco, CA 94109.

Library of Congress Cataloging-in-Publication Data

Feininger, Andreas, 1906–
    In a grain of sand.

    1. Natural history—Miscellanea. 2. Nature
(Aesthetics)   I. Title.
QH45.5.F45   1986   508   86–6431
ISBN 0–87156–763–6

Printed and bound in Italy by Amilcare Pizzi, S.p.A., Milan.

10 9 8 7 6 5 4 3 2 1

All photographs on pages 34–35, 36–37, 38–39, 40–41, 43, 45, 48, 49, 54, 62, 82, 83, 106, 107, 108, 109, 141, 142, 144, 145, 146, 150, and 151 were produced on assignment for Life Magazine and are copyrighted by Time Incorporated. They are published here with the permission of Time Inc.

Frontispiece: *The broken columella of a conch shell stands against the sky, reminiscent of baroque pillars, possibly inspired by the conch's spiraling design.*

This book is dedicated to Joan Baez
as a token of thanks—for the pleasure of her voice and beauty,
her humaneness, her indomitable spirit.

Contents

Foreword

To see a world in a grain of sand,
And a heaven in a wild flower,
Hold infinity in the palm of your hand,
And eternity in an hour.
William Blake (1757–1827)

In four short lines, this eloquent poem succeeds in evoking images that range from the crash of breaking waves to flowering meadows in spring; from boundless skies and eagles soaring over mountain peaks to memories of timeless bliss; from walks along a lonely beach to watching the wheeling stars.

I savor the beauty of each line and dwell on the important words: a world, a grain of sand; heaven and a flower; infinity and eternity. I let my mind go blank and give my thoughts free rein. A grain of sand—how could one see a world in a speck of dust? Then, out of the subconscious, questions rise: what is a grain of sand? where does it come from? what is its place in the cyclic drama of nature?

Sand is a loose sediment normally consisting of rounded particles of quartz. Quartz is silicone dioxide, SiO_2, a hard, usually colorless mineral. But what else is sand?

It is this: whenever I think of sand, two images rise before my inner eye—wide, sunny beaches, and the towering red sandstone cliffs of Utah and Colorado. Both are connected with some of the happiest moments in my life. Thinking of sand always puts me in a good mood: sunbathing by the sea; hand-in-hand with a lovely companion racing down the dunes into the foaming waves when life was still shiny and new; listening to the sound of the surf, the greatest symphony on earth; resting in the cool shade of soaring sandstone cliffs in our arid Southwest.

I take a handful of sun-warmed sand and let it run through my fingers. Where did it come from? What made the sand? I know that sand is all that is left of vanished mountains, the ultimate remains of rising cliffs and towering crags—a memento of the transient nature of life, the rocks, the earth, the stars. This clean, wave-washed sand was once massive rock of ancient mountains, rising miles perhaps into the sky. But sheared away by wind and frost, leveled from their heights by rain and gravity, rocks and mineral debris descended, collecting at the mountain's base and spilling out upon the valley floor in the form of great alluvial fans. In the blistering sun, this debris quickly dried, was further pulverized by falling rocks and erosion, swept by wind and rain into streams and rivers that ground it finer still, and eventually was carried to the sea and deposited, century after century, millennium after millennium, in the form of mile-long beds of sand—our dunes and beaches.

At other times, the unconsolidated sediments slowly sank deeper and deeper and were buried under the enormous weight of newer and newer layers of sand. Intense pressure coupled with mineralized solutions compacted and cemented the individual grains to form rock—sandstone—which, in the course of eons, uplifted by tectonic forces, became the core of a new generation of mountains. But nothing is permanent, and, in turn, these mountains were, or are going to be, leveled again by erosion and ground by running water into sand, only to rise once more in a never ending cycle of renewal and annihilation, of birth and death. Thus, through the power of the imagination, contemplating a grain of sand can evoke majestic visions: a single grain of sand can symbolize a world.

Another thought occurs to me: how did the *first* mountains originate?

This touches on fundamental questions about the origins of the earth that can be answered only speculatively by cosmologists. This is what scientists believe today: In the beginning, billions of years ago, there was what the great astrophysicist George Gamow called "the cosmic egg"—an immense fireball consisting of some superdense material that was not matter as we know it today but some unimaginable form of pure energy. This cosmic egg blew up in a cataclysmic explosion appropriately called the Big Bang, scattering particles and radiation in all directions at incomprehensible speeds and at temperatures of billions of degrees. This was the birth-pang of the Universe, the beginning of the galaxies and stars we see today—of the megagalactic system of which the earth and its mountains form only a microscopically insignificant part.

But still my mind is not satisfied because, inevitably, another question presents itself: how did this cosmic egg originate? On this point, science is mute, and many people are content to believe it was created by God. But, in that case, who or what created God?

There is another possibility, though. Today, perhaps the most hotly disputed question among cosmologists is whether our expanding universe will continue to expand forever—until the galaxies vanish beyond the rim of infinity—or whether the rate of expansion will gradually decrease due to gravitational forces, come to a halt, and the process reverse itself to end in a cataclysmic collapse. So far, the observational evidence for either theory is inconclusive. But it seems that there may be proof to support the latter hypothesis. For, if the cosmic egg really existed (and there seems to be very little doubt about this), couldn't it have been the result of the collapse of a previous universe—that ultimate collapse of the cosmos into a single fireball that the theory of the pulsating universe demands? The nucleus from which a new universe could rise—analogous to the myth of the phoenix, that gorgeous bird, which, having lived for several hundred years, burns itself to death in order to regain its youth, rise from the ashes, and live through another cycle?

What images, what vistas—beaches, rocks, and mountains; the earth, the galaxies, the universe; the cosmic egg and God—all evoked by the contemplation of a single grain of sand.

Thus, in Blake's poem, a grain of sand, an apparently insignificant object, becomes the symbol of concepts that are immense. Any number of other apparently insignificant objects and events in nature reveal themselves upon closer examination to be of equal significance—leaves, for example, or insects or coral or shells. What could be less imposing than a leaf? And yet, without green leaves, all animal life on earth would cease, including human life. After all, that magic substance, chlorophyll, a combination of water, carbon dioxide, and sunlight, produces the sugars that sustain all the plants and all the plant-eating creatures on earth, from aphids and grasshoppers to elephants and humans. And it is the plant-eating animals that in turn provide the food for the flesh eaters. Not only do leaves provide food, directly or indirectly, for all living things, but, in the process of manufacturing the life-sustaining dextroses, they also release oxygen, without which life as we know it cannot exist. And if ever we humans were foolish enough, deliberately or accidentally, to destroy a large percentage of all the plants, we and all the other animals would perish.

But what about the importance of insects? What could be lower or less significant than a "bug"—a hornet, a fly, an ant? Although many people may believe that if we could exterminate all the insects we could create a better world—a world free from mosquitoes, flies, and pests, a world free from insect-borne diseases such as malaria, rickettsia, yellow fever, sleeping sickness, and cholera, free from insect damage to farm crops, vegetables, and fruits—the price would be staggering: a world devoid of flowering plants, most of which depend on pollination by insects for their continuing existence. And a very large number of birds and other animals who feed on insects would also become extinct. No matter how "insignificant" an insect may appear to us, a world without them would be a drab and impoverished world, diminished in color, devoid of bird song, cheerless without the beauty and fragrance of flowers.

Corals are tiny animals half the size of a pea, and shells are mollusks—lime-encased blobs of animated slime. These seemingly insignificant corals build entire island chains, and mollusks create some of the most beautiful objects in nature—shells highly prized by collectors, living embodiments of mathematical formulas, which, considering their precision of execution, and functional and ornamental beauty, rival the most inspired works of man. "Grains of Sand . . ."

"And a heaven in a wild flower . . ." is another eloquent phrase of great symbolic power. To me, "heaven" stands for beauty, perfection, and joy, a state of inner harmony and grace. And flowers symbolize beauty, fragrance, and color. No wonder we give flowers to express sympathy, appreciation, sorrow, or love. And flowers can be found everywhere, free to be enjoyed by anyone who has an eye for beauty. Like leaves, insects, corals, and shells, flowers are "insignificant," all-pervading, and as common as "grains of sand." And yet, similar to these other objects of nature, they represent some of the most valuable resources of our world—in this case, a never ending wellspring of joy.

"Infinity" and "eternity" are concepts the true significance of which eludes the power of the human mind. Nobody can conceive of something going on and on forever, whether in terms of time or of space. Ultimately, there has to be an end, a goal, a halt. But in that case, what lies beyond?

But precisely because they surpass my ability to comprehend, the concepts "infinity" and "eternity" have a special fascination for me. They stand for something greater than I, greater than arrogant, self-centered people, greater even than the vaunted human brain. This quest for something transcending the self reflects a universal need of humanity. Some people satisfy this urge by creating and worshiping gods. Others, like myself, are still searching. Although I may never arrive at a final conclusion, the fact that something exists forever beyond my intellectual grasp is strangely reassuring. I don't know what it is, but I know it exists: call it the Essence, the Mystery, the All. Nameless and indefinable, it manifests itself in the force that joins atom to atom, organizes galaxies, and rules the motions of the stars. It makes plants and trees grow upright, defying the force of gravity, and encapsulates the secret of life in a seed. It converts caterpillars into butterflies. It tells a spider how to spin its complicated web and birds how to construct their nests. It enables us to create music, poetry, and art. It transforms common matter into bird song and the fragrance of flowers. It is the essence of life.

This book evolved from a sense of wonder, the sense of wonder of a child who has discovered something new and marvelous, not knowing or caring whether other people might have made the same discovery before, enjoying what he found with admiration, reverence, and awe.

My attitude toward nature has survived since my childhood and only grew stronger and more consciously defined with age. This attitude saw beauty and meaning in objects as simple and insignificant as bugs and leaves and stones. Later, after I learned more about such things, I found out that my intuitive feelings had been right—flowers, for example, cannot exist without pollinating bugs, and leaves are the indispensable basis of life.

And then, some time ago, a friend to whom I had given a copy of my book *Roots of Art* (Viking, 1975) saw in it an affinity to Blake's poem "To see the world in a grain of sand. . . ," and lightning struck: this was precisely what I had felt all along, the spirit in which I had approached all objects of nature. Suddenly, everything fell into place. I no longer felt alone. My courage returned, and with it my enthusiasm that had been in danger of being stifled by frustration resulting from apathy on the part of most people toward things that mattered most to me.

Today, people generally are better educated than at any other time in history. Yet it seems sometimes that, although they know more, they give less thought to what they know. For example, most people know about the marvels of the human body. Yet they abuse their bodies in the most horrendous ways, undermining their health with excessive use of alcohol and tobacco, with drugs, by overeating, and by lack of exercise. Likewise, the dangers to our very existence resulting from overpopulation and pollution of the environment are on the minds of most informed people. Yet only a tiny minority work actively toward a solution. The vast majority—as proven by the way they vote and select their representatives for Congress—prefer not to rock the boat, to avoid anything that might interfere with their profits, affect their personal comfort, or upset their religious beliefs, even though the consequences for future generations might be disastrous. Such people do not use their knowledge. The knowledge is wasted, as valueless as a reference library not used, books not read, or photographs not seen. This is the difference between knowledge and awareness: knowledge is hoarded money, awareness is money spent wisely or invested with care. It is the purpose of this book to help transform knowledge into awareness. Reading the text and contemplating the following photographs may not add significantly to the reader's knowledge but will, I hope, make him or her increasingly aware of the significance and beauty of some of the objects and phenomena that surround us.

The images in this book show common objects of nature that caught my eye and interest. Despite its random appearance, this picture collection is unified by a single thought: meaning and beauty exist in every object of nature. Nothing is truly "insignificant." If only we have eyes to see and minds to contemplate, these manifestations of nature can enrich our lives by their aesthetic appeal and by increasing our awareness of our surroundings, our world, ourselves.

Although some of the following photographs may look fantastic, all are "real" insofar as all are straight, unmanipulated pictures of the respective objects. These objects were, of course, arranged in ways that suited my purpose, which was to stimulate the viewers and make them see, feel, and think in a manner they hadn't experienced before. To achieve this, I made full use of the camera's creative potential. I magnified some objects, eliminated all indications of scale, and thereby made it possible to turn a rock into a mountain. I changed perspective and viewpoint at will; increased or decreased, wherever I deemed necessary, the contrast between light and dark; selected or rejected my subjects in accordance with artistic demands, and put emphasis where emphasis belonged. Despite such artistic license, everything I show is real: real leaves, rocks, shells, beach sand, clouds, and skies, brought together in specific, previsualized configurations through the magic of photography.

In aggregate, these images are the tangible expression of my belief that everything in nature is "designed." Designing means giving form in accordance with specific requirements or causes; it also implies the presence of a designer. In nature, the designer is the totality of cosmic forces, which manifest themselves in three main forms: electromagnetic forces, gravitational effects, and subatomic forces.

Electromagnetic forces (light, radiant heat, electricity, magnetism) make life possible on earth by raising the average temperature of our planet above the freezing point of water (water in liquid form is an indispensable requirement of life) and providing the energy without which plants could not exist. Without plants, there could be no animals because only plants are able to synthesize food out of inorganic matter through photosynthesis: with chlorophyll providing the machinery and light the energy, six molecules of carbon dioxide combine with six of water to produce one molecule of sugar and six of oxygen. It is this single molecule of sugar, multiplied by the unimaginable number of such molecules synthesized continuously throughout most of the world on land and in the sea, which is the basis of life: plant-eating animals feed on grass or leaves, flesh-eating animals feed on animals that fed on plants. The steak you eat tonight is nothing but converted plant matter, which, in turn, is mostly carbon dioxide from the air and water from the ground enriched with a few minerals "cooked" by sunlight. And it is the oxygen liberated during photosynthesis that made the air fit to breathe for animals and humans because, before the advent of plants, the original atmosphere contained no oxygen but consisted primarily of water vapor, hydrogen, nitrogen, methane, and ammonia—some of which spell death to animal life. Hence, in the last analysis, all living things, animals as well as plants, owe their existence to, and are largely designed by, electromagnetic forces.

Gravity is the force that powers the tides and makes water run downhill, carving gullies, canyons, and valleys into the stony surface of the land, designing its major features. It is gravity that makes plants and trees grow upright seeking light and sends roots downward seeking water. It is gravity that dictates the maximum size of animals and plants and thereby prevents them from collapsing under their own weight. It is gravity that keeps our feet firmly planted on the ground and keeps the earth in its path around the sun, preventing both humanity and planet from being catapulted into deadly interstellar space.

Subatomic forces weld atom to atom and thus establish form. They also fuel the heat machinery of the earth, float the continents on molten rock and indirectly cause volcanism and earthquakes, thereby contributing to the "design" of many terrestrial features.

None of these three primary forces, of course, is exclusively responsible for the shape of things. They interact, each contributing its share. The ramifications are infinite. Consider, for example, the sun, earth's own "personal" star: it provides us with gravity, light, and heat—indispensable requirements for life—and in countless ways, directly or indirectly, shapes the design of inanimate matter as well as that of living things. Solar heat causes water to evaporate from the seas, eventually to come down as rain (by gravity), to be taken up by plants, which subsequently might be eaten by animals, which in turn could become food for flesh eaters. Air currents induced by thermal solar radiation modified by geological features determine which parts of the land will get much and which will get little rainfall, creating environments from rainforests to deserts. The character of these different environments in turn is reflected in the shape of the animals and plants that inhabit them as well as in their terrestrial features: gullies cut by running water, dunes of windblown sand, plants and animals adapted to extremes of wetness or dryness, heat or cold. All of these can in the last analysis trace their design back to the sun.

Besides the three primary forces cited above, a number of secondary factors exist that influence design in nature. The most important ones are light, temperature, water, winds, and self-preservation.

Light—or its absence—affects the habits and therefore the design of many animals and plants. All plants grow toward the light—sensitivity to light is part of their design. When darkness falls, many day-blooming plants close their flowers to protect the precious pollen from being damaged by dew. And the flowers of night-blooming plants are white to provide maximum visibility in the dark to pollinating moths. Nocturnal animals need more sensitive (which means larger) eyes than diurnal ones. Animals living in eternal darkness—in the ground or in deep caves—have no use for eyes and lost them in the course of evolution. Most day-flying butterflies are brightly colored; most night-flying moths are drab, since in darkness color no longer exists and coloration becomes useless.

Temperature. Life, that enigmatic force, is able to adapt to environments whose temperatures range from nearly boiling point to way below freezing: living organisms can be found in the hot pools surrounding geysers in Yellowstone

National Park and in the shimmering summer heat of Death Valley as well as in the bone-chilling wastes of the Arctic. To thrive under such extremes of heat and cold, the respective organisms had to be "designed" accordingly, that is, endowed with special features that counteract the life-threatening effects of extreme temperatures. Well-known examples are penguins, seals, and polar bears; cacti, yuccas, and creosote bushes. The main characteristics of their "design"—the peculiarities that distinguish them from animals and plants found in more temperate regions, the features that ensure their survival where more "ordinary" life forms could not exist—were "designed" by temperature.

Water, as a creative force, is one of the most powerful and universal of all "designers" in nature. Water streamlined the fishes and led to the development of the gill, gave ducks and geese their webbed feet, and enabled whales to reach their monstrous, gravity-defying size. Amazingly, in water, properly designed objects are weightless, no matter how heavy they are on land. And it is water, through erosion, that has created all the valleys on earth—V-shaped in cross section if carved by running water, U-shaped if gouged in ancient times by ice. In the course of this work, water carries billions of tons of sand and rocky debris from high points to lowlands and finally into the sea. In the course of eons, then, it levels mountains, forms plains, and, through oceanic sedimentation followed by uplift, creates new land and mountains again. Since water is one of the indispensable requirements of life, its scarcity, as in arid regions, produces specially adapted forms of plants and animals with design features that enable them to get along with minimum amounts of the precious liquid. Absence of water precludes life.

Wind, as a designing force, plays both a constructive and a destructive role in nature. In its destructive mode, wind whips up waves that can change coast lines, erode beaches, undermine cliffs, and tumble boulders into the surf, where rock, grinding against rock, is soon pulverized to sand, forming the material for new beaches. Striking dry land, storms can erode its surface, carry away millions of tons of topsoil, thereby destroying its fertility, leaving "dust bowls." Hurricanes and tornadoes cut swaths of destruction across the land. In its constructive mode, wind powers windmills, generators, sailboats, and is indispensable for the pollination of many plants such as the evergreens—the pines, firs, spruces, redwoods, and so on—the maples, the oaks, the poplars and birches, ragweed, and a host of other plants, all of which are specifically designed for wind pollination. It also is the distributing agent for the seeds of plants such as dandelions, milkweed, thistles, goldenrod, and the maples and ashes, all of which developed specific seed forms designed to facilitate this process: gossamer parachutes, or fine propellerlike blades that whirl the seed point-first toward the ground.

Self-preservation is one of the most powerful of all life drives, stronger than sex and hunger, equalled, and occasionally surpassed, only by love. As a designing force of nature, it has produced untold variations and modifications of a few basic designs in animals and plants—for example, the mammals. Basically, all mammals consist of a compact body, a head at one end, a tail at the other, and four legs. Yet how many different versions of this basic design exist? From moles to mastodons, hares to horses, bats to boars—each possesses specific anatomic and behavioral qualities designed to enable it to take fullest advantage of its particular niche in the great web of life. Many of these qualities are very specific, not to say genial, adaptations, such as the huge digging front feet of the mole, the trunk of the mastodon, the wings of the bat, the murderous tusks of the warthog, the spines of porcupines—design features evolved in order to give their owners a better chance in life; they are tangible manifestations of the principle of self-preservation. And the same holds true for plants. The tough, leathery epidermis and the vicious spines of cacti are their means to increase their chances for survival in a hostile environment, as are the stinging hairs of nettles, the skin-blistering oil of poison ivy, the thorns of roses, raspberry, barberry bush. Intricate mechanisms of pollination are designed to force insects to play their indispensable role. In the last analysis, every single feature of animals and plants that distinguishes one species from another results from a modification of one basic form in the interest of self-preservation, whether accomplished under the pressure of light, temperature, water, or wind. As a result, the number of design features that owe their existence to the force of self-preservation is virtually infinite.

In nature, every form is the direct or indirect outcome of a force that caused the respective "design" to come into being, whether this form is part of an inanimate object or a living thing. But what is life? Where does it begin? Where does it end? Where do we draw the line between the animate and the inanimate, provided a clear-cut boundary exists? Obviously, a barking dog is alive, whereas the rocks beside a road are not. But matters are not always that simple. Let's analyze the body of a living dog, for example. It contains organs such as heart, lungs, liver, and so on, which consist of tissues, which in turn are composed of cells—all unquestionably "alive." But as we go further down the line, things become confused. The "living" cells, for example, consist of molecules, which are aggregations of atoms, which in turn consist of subatomic particles such as protons, neutrons, electrons, and so on. The atoms themselves are representations of elements—for example, carbon, oxygen, calcium, iron, copper, and zinc. These elements are inanimate matter, and so must be the molecules that they form. How, then, can cells be "alive" if the matter of which they consist is "dead"? Is there a special force that at some point interferes and infuses dead matter with life? Is this idea analogous to a gasoline engine, where the energy from a battery, activating the starter to turn the crankshaft, which drives the fuel pump and the distributor and the camshaft, which opens and closes the valves so that gasoline can enter the cylinders and ignite, eventually brings the motor to life? Despite an intensive search, though, not the slightest indication of such a life force has ever been found.

The alternative is a startling notion: Everything from humans to stone is "alive." There is no sharp dividing line separating the animate from the inanimate, only degrees of animation.

The unique characteristics of life are growth, metabolism, reproduction, and the power of adaptation to the environment. Despite these stringent specifications, clearly there are different degrees or levels of life: the life of a person is more complex than a frog's, which in turn is a more complex creature than an oyster. And the life of any vertebrate—animals having a brain—is totally different from that of a tree—a plant without a brain or even a nervous system. Yet despite this enormous difference, both are able to "feel"—they react to outside stimulants: plants are sensitive to gravity, light, temperature, humidity, touch (several species fold their leaves upon being touched), and acidity, even though they cannot "think." Even bacteria are unquestionably alive. And viruses, those ultramicroscopic infectious agents, those "living molecules" that can reproduce only in living cells, are they also alive? At this level, distinction begins to blur: viruses, when desiccated, disintegrate into a uniform powder just as minerals do, losing all attributes of life. Yet when injected into a suitable host cell, this powder almost miraculously reconstructs itself into the same kind of virus from which it came, resuming its previous "life."

With regard to growth, metabolism, reproduction, and adaptation—are they really qualities restricted to life? Perhaps these "unique characteristics of life" also manifest themselves in different degrees. Growth, for example, is equivalent to organized increase in volume—a phenomenon we find not only in animals and plants, but also in the mineral kingdom, where crystals grow precisely in this fashion. Metabolism is basically a process in which energy is produced. It is a fact that certain chemicals, when brought into contact, produce heat—a form of energy. Reproduction means duplication, copying—a process that constantly goes on at the molecular level during growth of living organisms. Under certain conditions, "dead" molecules are able to duplicate themselves. Adaptation is the power to adjust to specific conditions. This occurs during crystallization and dendrite formation: quartz crystals lining the inside of a geode, for example, adapt themselves to its inner surface configuration, and mineralized solutions crystallizing in cracks in rock often assume the form of dendrites—clearly organized, plant-like structures whose individual branches never cross or even touch one another. In other words, they don't behave as one might expect an inorganic substance to do—in a random fashion—but develop in such a manner that each branch and branchlet adapts itself to the whole so that overlapping and even contact are strictly avoided, almost as if the whole structure—the dendrite—could "think" and grow in accordance with a preconceived plan. Why this is so is not known.

All this seems to indicate that, to varying degrees, *everything* is alive, from humans, animals, and plants down to stones and atoms. Rocks are not "dead" in the sense that they are devoid of inner activity. On the contrary, their atoms are in a constant state of excitation, vibrating, their electrons whirling around their nuclei, their radioactive components disintegrating spontaneously, releasing heat. Some minerals can even "feel"—they react to outside stimuli just as animals and plants do. Iron, for example, is sensitive to magnetism, and when exposed to moisture, it responds by rusting. Selenium and silver halides are sensitive to light. Water strongly reacts to temperature—it freezes or turns to steam. Aren't reactions like these indications that we are dealing with some forms of life?

If this sounds fantastic—I agree. But more and more frequently, science has shown us that things are not what they seem to be. The sun is not the center of the universe, nor does it circle the earth. There is a limit to speed—the velocity of light. Space is curved. Black holes in interstellar space swallow everything in their vicinity including light. Apparently solid objects are mostly empty space because the distances between their atoms are relatively enormous. Energy can be converted to other forms, including matter, but cannot be destroyed.

On a more modest scale, here is another poser: horizontal lines are not straight but curved, and vertical ones are not parallel but divergent. That this is so becomes evident when one visualizes a globe: horizontal lines follow the curvature of the earth and therefore must be curves. Vertical lines are at right angles to horizontal ones and therefore cannot be parallel—they converge toward the center of the earth.

Modern cosmological thought tends toward simplification and unification—one grand equation applying to every physical phenomenon in the universe. In this sense—seen as part of a gigantic puzzling whole—the idea that *everything* is alive seems no longer strange, certainly no stranger than the concepts of infinity and eternity, which, to the human mind, are totally incomprehensible (although mathematicians and cosmologists deal with them all the time, they, too, cannot ''understand'' them). We simply cannot grasp anything that has neither beginning nor end. If space and time actually have a beginning and an end, we then ask, what came before? What comes afterwards? And does this ''before'' and ''after'' have a beginning and an end, too?

As energy can only be converted but not destroyed, so life is indestructible. A person, an animal, a tree may ''die,'' but I feel that death is only a transitional phase in an eternal cycle. The substance of the dead dissociates into its basic components, returns to the earth, the water, the air, only to be taken up again by other organisms—bacteria, fungi, animals, absorbed by the roots of plants—in a vast recycling process in which nothing is ever lost and everything is used again . . . and again . . . and again. The carbon atoms in my body may once have been part of a sigillaria tree in a carboniferous swamp, a dinosaur, a mammoth, or an ice-age woman or man; they will, after my death, become components of other living creatures again.

Q. AND A.

Q. Do you really believe that both a barking dog and a stone are alive since they are so enormously different? The dog can run around and move under its own power while the stone cannot; the dog can bark while the stone is eternally silent; the dog can reproduce while the stone cannot; the dog must eventually die while the stone can last indefinitely. I think the whole idea is absurd.

A. Don't get me wrong. I never said that a dog and a stone possess the same kind of life; I said that there are different degrees of aliveness. Take, for example, a tree or a colony of corals. Both are unquestionably alive, yet neither one can move under its own power, and both are eternally silent, just like the stone. Here we are dealing with a different kind of aliveness from that of a dog—life at a somewhat lower level.

Q. OK, but both the tree and the colony of coral can reproduce, while the stone cannot. How do you intend to bridge *that* difference?

A. I believe that viruses provide the answer. In their active stage, viruses show many of the qualities of life; desiccated, they appear as "dead" as any chemical powder. Viruses are unable to reproduce as are stones but must depend in this respect on living cells of the proper kind, which they invade and program to produce viruses instead of their own kind of cells when they divide. In other words, viruses represent a form of life that straddles what traditionally is considered "alive" and what is called "inanimate." They are the link between the world of animals and plants on one side and that of stone on the other.

Q. Hm . . . perhaps . . . but there still remains the fact that dogs, trees, and corals sooner or later die while stones exist indefinitely. I feel this is what makes the real difference between what is alive and what is inanimate.

A. The way I see it, death is an event that connects two different states, or levels, of existence. Before death, a "living" organism can maintain itself; after death, it loses this capacity and disintegrates into its basic components—chemical compounds, molecules, atoms. In other words, it makes what might be called a quantum leap from a high level of life to a lower one. However, the components of a "dead" animal or plant continue to live their own kind of life (being now at the lowest level of aliveness) but can at any time become food for compound organisms such as bacteria, fungi, plants, or animals and thereby become part of a higher order of aliveness again.

You said that "a stone can exist indefinitely." This is not true. You only have to look at stone in the city. It corrodes, it flakes off, it crumbles under the onslaught of acid rain, sulphur-laden smoke, frost, and other destructive forces. In open country, stone weathers, erodes, and is swept away by running water grain by grain. In other words, it disintegrates, decomposes, and dies. The same, of course, is true of mountains. They, too, are gradually leveled by the forces of erosion, and the reason they seem to us "eternal" is that this process takes time—time measured in millions of years. The changes that occur during the span of a human life are simply too small to be noticeable except, perhaps, with the aid of the most sophisticated scientific instruments.

Q. I still think you are nuts.

A. That's what people traditionally thought of everybody who came up with a theory that seemed to violate cherished beliefs. But philosophically speaking, the idea that there is a transition—instead of a break—between things traditionally called alive and those considered inanimate is very appealing to me. It also seems to be more in accordance with other natural phenomena as well as with the latest scientific thinking (as I mentioned before), in the same sense that the theory of evolution has replaced that of catastrophism. Give it some thought.

SOME THOUGHTS ABOUT DESIGN

The term "design" has several denotations: plan, pattern, organization, composition, intention, purpose, end.

To me, a former architect and structural engineer, any kind of design—design in the broadest sense of the term—has always had a special fascination. As I see it, *everything* is "designed," either by the brain and hand of humans or by the forces of nature. Studying, analyzing, and comparing with one another these different kinds of design is a source of never ending pleasure and stimulation.

One of the results of this preoccupation with design has been the realization that on countless occasions nature has anticipated human invention: birds, bats, and insects knew how to fly millions of years before man designed the first flying machine; the hip preceded the ball-and-socket joint, the elbow joint preceded the hinge. Bats and whales developed echolocating systems based on sound long before Sonar was invented. Feathers, in regard to specific gravity and thermal insulation power, still surpass any synthetic substance. The tensile strength of spiderweb silk per unit weight exceeds that of structural steel. And so on.

Another result of my interest in design was the realization that, in nature, *every* form of *everything*, whether inanimate or alive, is the tangible manifestation of either a definite cause (in the case of inanimate matter), or a specific purpose (if living organisms are involved), whereas the design of an artifact is often only vaguely related to its purpose because it is dominated, sometimes in flagrant disregard of practical consequences, by aesthetic considerations. A field where this is particularly often the case is automotive design, where the layout of the dashboard and the design of its instruments are frequently unsatisfactory—impractical, ineffective, pretentious and confusing to the point of being potentially dangerous—and all this in the name of "beauty." Another field where practical demands are often subordinated to aesthetic appeal is that of handles and knobs. Especially objectionable examples can be found among bathroom faucet knobs, coffeemaker handles, frying pan handles, and knobs on furniture, all of whose sharp edges, proximity to hot surfaces, or ornamental embellishments make them a daily source of annoyance. Similar feelings can also be evoked by chair designs, which sacrifice comfort to aesthetic pretensions.

In contrast to such misguided efforts, the designs of nature are always superbly effective and often breathtakingly beautiful. Bad, that is to say, ineffective, design doesn't exist in nature for the simple reason that it would be quickly eliminated by the struggle for existence. A considerable part of the pleasure I derive from contemplating nature's designs stems from their competence, which evokes my admiration and respect.

Design implies both *structural* arrangement (three-dimensional organization) and *surface* pattern (two-dimensional organization). In the following picture section I'll show examples of both.

To execute her designs, Nature employs two methods: *construction* and *reduction*—adding and taking away. This is analogous to the sculptor who also has the choice of two techniques: he or she can execute, say, a portrait head either by accretion—by adding clay to clay—or by reduction—by chipping away at a marble block to free the form that already exists in the mind. In nature, the first method is equivalent to *growth*—adding layer to layer as in sediments, ring to ring as in tree growth, molecule to molecule as in the growing of animals, plants, and crystals—*construction*. The second method corresponds to *deterioration*—reduction, dissolution, decrease and loss of substance through the influence of external forces such as running water, frost, wind, or decay—*destruction*.

Nature's designs can be classified in one of two categories: *planned* and *fortuitous*.

We find *planned design* in the human form and in the forms of animals and plants that are more or less predictable: we know the kind of shape a Doberman puppy will develop into and we know what will come out of a sunflower seed. Similarly, the form that the crystals of specific minerals will take is predictable. This kind of design is "planned" because it is inherent in the nature of the thing, latent already in the genes of animals and plants and the atomic structure of minerals. This kind of design is the product of *internal* forces.

On the other hand, *fortuitous design* is more or less unpredictable and often accidental. We know that running water can gully the land and carve out valleys, but we cannot predict precisely how, when, and where such an event will take place. This kind of design is seen in the results of erosion, wave action, frost, and wind. Examples of it are broken shells (despite their small size, they can have forms as powerful as great sculpture), pebbles ground to symmetrical perfection by the surf, erosion patterns in silt or clay, ripple marks in sand, and so on. This kind of design is the product of *external* forces.

On my desk, in front of me, rests the bleached skull of a gull, which I found not long ago on a beach. Picked clean of skin and flesh by crabs, it is an object of exquisite beauty—so delicate, feather-light to the point of weightlessness, its components paper-thin yet tough enough to have withstood the battering of breaking waves without breaking.

To me, this skull is only one of the countless miracles of natural design—a "miracle" in two respects: its perfection as a functional part of a gull's design, and the way it came into being.

The smooth, unbroken line from the tip of the beak to the top of the skull reflects the streamlined body of a bird designed to part the air in soaring, effortless flight. The bones are thin enough to be translucent, and since weight is the greatest enemy of any airborne design, mass is further reduced by leaving holes in places where structural considerations permit this—holes that also serve as passages for nerves. No human engineer aided by a computer could have produced a better design.

The fact that this admirable object has actually constructed itself borders on the miraculous. Complete "blueprints" for the construction, not only of this skull but of an entire gull—including minutely detailed specifications regarding all the necessary materials, instructions for their use, and sequence of assembly—are already contained in the genes of the parent birds. These microscopic units of heredity, these specks of living matter too small to be seen by the naked eye, contain millions of "bits" of information encoded in groups of atoms, which, in due time, in some unfathomable way, will result in the "construction" of a living gull, fish, dog, elephant, or human being.

Imagine the astronomical number of "instructions" encoded in a fertilized egg cell smaller than the dot above the letter "i," containing everything needed to "construct" a caterpillar, which will transform itself into a butterfly with its colorful wing designs composed of thousands of microscopically small scales, each in its proper place, each executed to perfection; or a bird complete to the most minute detail of its smallest feather; or a 50-ton whale. Or the ultimate marvel, a human being with all its organs, each unimaginably complex in itself—a brain able to experience emotions, beauty, music, art . . . a mind capable of sending men to the moon and sounding the secrets of the universe; a heart that ceaselessly pumps blood for 80 years; eyes constructed so incredibly precise that they can distinguish between the different wave lengths of light and let us see and enjoy color; the various glands, chemical factories infinitely more complex than any built by humans, which produce the hundreds of different enzymes and hormones without which we could not live; the nervous system; lungs and liver and kidneys and stomach and intestines; the reproductive organs, which can replicate an entire living being. All this magic is contained in the ovum in chains of molecules, which in time will unfold and grow, nurtured by food created by plants out of inorganic matter energized by the sun, food that may have been transformed from grass to animal flesh to mother's milk to feed a baby, which, grown to maturity, can keep the cycle going, perpetuating the race, without end.

I give my thoughts free rein and see a world alive with mystery and wonder. Wherever I turn I see design, from the cone of a volcano raised by tectonic forces to the tiny conelike mounds thrown up by burrowing wasps. I find the mystic ratio of the Golden Section encoded in the Fibonacci numbers and these again embodied in the structural design of many plants. I see the spiral design repeated in the swirling star clouds of galaxies, in the arrangement of the blossoms of Queen Anne's lace, and in the shells of mollusks. For over 40 years I have recorded nature's designs with my camera and published what I found in several picture books. But as I kept on working, seeing, and discovering, new images were born. I now want to share these pictures with you.

Andreas Feininger

IN A GRAIN OF SAND

I. The Land

Nothing is permanent, not even "eternal" mountains. Landscapes change with time just as people do. They seem changeless because the rate of transformation is usually so slow that the span of a human life is too short to let us notice the result. Only change is permanent.

Landscapes change under the influence of external and internal forces, the most powerful of which are volcanism, tectonic movement within the crust of the earth, running water, glaciers, frost, and wind. These are the great "designers" that ceaselessly transform the everchanging features of the land.

Volcanism is the force most likely to produce quick changes in the appearance of a landscape. Volcanoes such as Krakatoa, Vesuvius, Mount Pelee, and Mt. St. Helens have altered their immediate surroundings drastically, sometimes within hours.

Tectonic movement within the crust of the earth is the force that uplifts mountains. The Himalayas are the result of India, riding its own tectonic plate, driving into the Asiatic mainland with such force that it wrinkled it like a piece of cloth.

Running water or water frozen in the form of glaciers is the "designer" that created all the valleys, canyons, gorges, and gullies on earth, and, in the process, leveled mountains.

Frost lets water freeze in cracks, thereby splitting rocks and becoming an active contributor to erosion.

Glaciers gouge valleys out of bedrock, or, like giant carpenter's planes, during periods of glaciation, they level entire continents. After melting, they leave the rocky debris in the form of mountainous moraines.

Wind carries away dry topsoil, turns fertile land into dust bowls, and piles up sand in the form of ever-shifting dunes.

Each of these great forces leaves its stamp upon the land. Trying to figure out which influence caused which effect is a fascinating game that anyone interested can play after reading one of the basic books on geology and acquiring some knowledge. I have found that it contributes considerably to my enjoyment of outdoor life.

Volcanism gave Mt. Shasta (*above*), a 14,160-foot high volcano in the Cascade Range of northern California, its characteristic cone shape—a form as typical for volcanoes as it is for ant hills (*right*), except that in the first case the "designer" is a tectonic force, while in the second it is the combined effort of a colony of ants. Despite the enormous difference in size, both structures are manifestations of the interrelationship between function and form.

Water gave this Utah saltflat its characteristic look—the dry bottom of an ancient lake. During the last Ice Age, a climate wetter than the present one prevailed over much of the western United States, and lakes formed in many of the intermontane

basins. Some 10,000 to 12,000 years ago, however, the climate turned warmer and drier, and the lakes gradually disappeared through evaporation. Their desiccated beds now form these remarkably flat and featureless plains.

A glacier gouged out the valley of Maligne Lake in Jasper National Park in southwestern Alberta, Canada, during the last Ice Age, some 10,000 years ago.

Pages 38–39: Erosion on a gigantic scale created the Badlands of South Dakota. Such land formations are typical of terrains underlaid by weakly consolidated, flat-lying sedimentary rocks in semi-arid climates. The "designers" are rainfall, sheetwash, and stream erosion. The bizarre morphology of such landscapes is enhanced by the unequal resistance to weathering by the rock layers. The broad strips of low-lying flat areas are alluviated, ephemeral stream channels filled with the debris eroded and washed from the overlooking hills, ridges, and pinnacles. In a more humid climate, these forms would normally be smoothed and covered by a uniform mantle of vegetation.

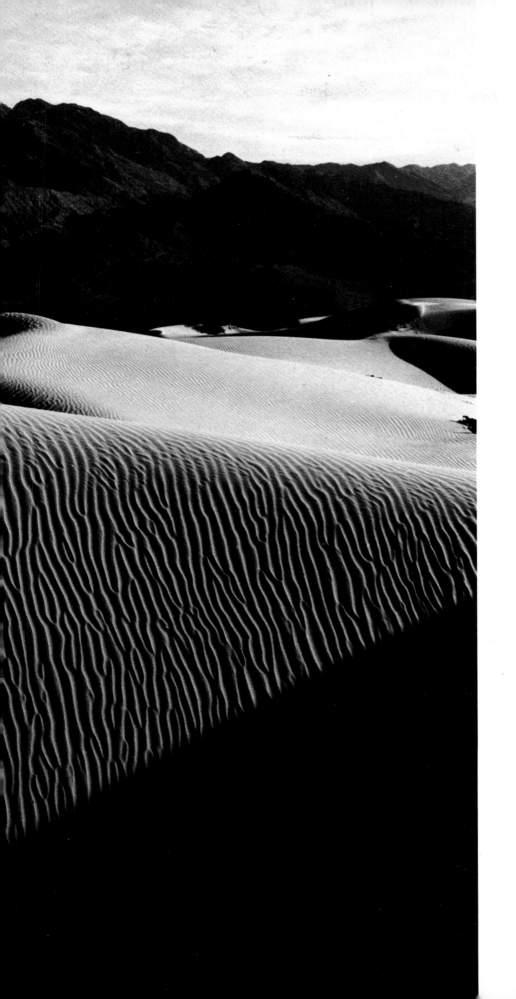

Wind gave these soft, sensuous sand dunes in California's Death Valley their appealing texture and shape—ephemeral structures that constantly shift with changes in wind and weather.

II. Wind and Water

The great designing forces of nature determine the overall character of a landscape and affect it down to its last detail. Volcanic mountains, for example, have that typical cone shape, which unmistakably spells "volcano" even if other signs have long since been blurred by time. After an eruption the entire environment is changed by lava and pumice covering the surface rocks, topsoil buried under layers of volcanic ash, and trees broken and burned. All these are unmistakable signs of volcanism.

The main evidence left by running water is surface erosion of the land. This can take many forms, from small runnels and narrow gullies to deep gorges and majestic canyons. Furthermore, boulders, stones, and pebbles are no longer sharp-edged but more or less rounded, polished even, by the tumbling force of running water in combination with the abrasive effect of the pulverized minerals carried by it. Any rounded pebble is irrefutable evidence of the action of running water.

That water tends to blur the edges of things is not confined to stones, driftwood, broken glass, and other inorganic objects but can be observed also in living things, such as in the "streamlining" of fishes. Nature, during millions of years of evolution, has eliminated all protruding body parts to make the smoothest possible passage of the fish's form through water. Here, too, water indirectly gave fish their characteristic "design."

Wind leaves its signature on the land mainly in the form of shifting dunes, "dust bowls," and changes in shorelines due to wave action resulting from wind—storms and hurricanes. And, as water "designed" fish, wind has indirectly "designed" numerous plants, whose reproductive mechanisms are adapted to and make use of the wind. Best known examples of this are dandelions, milkweed, thistles, and cottonwood, whose delicate, parachute-like seeds travel on currents of air to spread their kind. Also pine, spruce, hemlock, maple, and oak, besides ragweed and many other plants, grow inconspicuous flowers designed to be pollinated not by insects, but by wind.

Cirrocumulus clouds above the desert form an airy design, whose towering loftiness allegorizes the freedom of boundless space.

Water in the form of clouds and steam forms everchanging designs. *Above*: Vultures riding thermal updrafts float effortlessly on air in lofty weightlessness, spiraling higher and higher toward a deck of altostratus clouds above a desert highway, on the lookout for animals killed by cars. *Opposite*: In Yellowstone National Park a geyser, a sinter cone only a few feet high, looms mountainlike through clouds of steam.

Water in the form of ice and frost forms some of the most exquisite designs in nature. *Above*: Ice crystals on the windshield of a car left outdoors on a chilly winter night. *Opposite*: Frost pattern on a window pane; its bold and sweeping design brings to mind ferns and feathers, whose principle of structural organization is the same.

Erosion—the combined effects of water, frost, and wind—created these strange geological designs. *Above*: In Utah's Bryce Canyon, a capstone provides temporary protection to a pillar of conglomerate— a mixture of gravel and clay—which nevertheless is doomed to eventual collapse by erosion. *Opposite*: Eroded clay-and-gravel embankment. Its rhythmic pattern brings to mind the flying buttresses of gothic cathedrals.

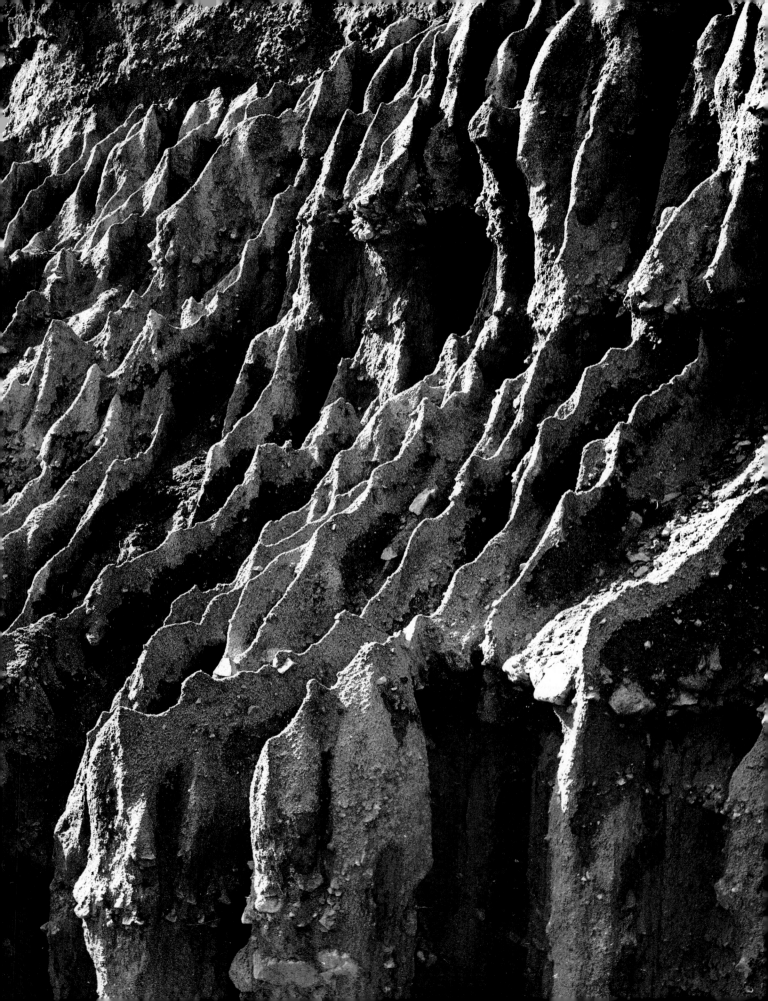

Arco di Constantino (*above*) and *Arco di Settimo Severo* (*opposite*), Rome. A closer look at these monuments dating back to Roman Imperial times reveals the effects of erosion on them: under the ceaseless onslaught by wind and rain, aided by industrial pollution, the edges soften, the sharp forms blur, the material crumbles, and the carved stone reverts in time to the shapelessness of natural weather-beaten rock.

Design by water would be a fitting caption for these photographs of sharks and water-worn pebbles. In both cases, water gave them their form. The "streamlined" shape of fish is the result of millions of years of evolution toward the most effortless propulsion through water, and the rounded, polished, beautifully symmetrical forms of the granite pieces ground to geometrical perfection are due to tumbling in the surf off Montauk Point, Long Island, N.Y.

Wind erosion left these clumps of hardy arrow weed stranded high
and dry on pillars of sand, precariously held together by their roots
while the surrounding desert floor is constantly lowered by erosion.

Wind—like a designer using a compass—draws circles on the desert floor, using the needle-tipped blades of hardy grasses as tools.

Ventrifacts—stones sculptured by wind action. I found these
beautifully carved specimens in the Mojave desert, where abrasive
sand driven by powerful winds had removed the softer particles first,
creating effects that may have been enhanced by leaching.

Milkweed—a plant whose dissemination is totally dependent on wind. *Opposite*: A seed capsule splits open, releasing a burst of seeds—a veritable symbol of the irrepressible power of life. *Above*: A single milkweed seed, parachute-equipped, floats gently to the ground.

III. Structure

Everything in nature has structure, is "constructed" in accordance with a specific "design." This is true not only of complex organisms such as the human body, but of every object of nature, from trees to single leaves, birds to feathers, mountains to rocks to grains of sand.

As a designer, an architect, and an engineer and fascinated by the interdependence of function and form, I find exploring, studying, and enjoying objects of nature a most rewarding pastime. It takes me away from the often oppressive details of daily life, satisfies my curiosity, challenges my analytical mind, and rewards me with insight into the workings of the cosmos which is spiritually uplifting, showing me my place as a humble human being in the grand design of Nature, and filling me with respect for her creations.

Walking in the forest I see slim vines of Virginia creeper cross my path and carefully avoid stepping on the tender leaves that are arranged along the stem in a regular, evenly spaced pattern—a "design." I halt at the stump of a tree felled by loggers and count the annual growth rings in the wood, which tell me the age of the tree at the time of its death and offer me glimpses into some aspects of its life: a wide ring speaks of a good year with plenty of rain and sunshine, a narrow one indicates drought or ravage by insects. The wood of this and most other trees is layered, its material deposited in a design that is an indicator of time, a kind of natural clock, a carrier of coded information. This form of design is also employed in the structure of clam shells, many minerals, and certain parts of the crust of the earth. Trying to decipher these codes to learn about the past is a challenge that has been taken up again and again by some of our best minds.

Continuing my walk I constantly have to slow my steps—there is so much to see, so much to think about, to enjoy. I pick up a leaf and admire its construction, the skeleton of conductive veins that stiffen its paper-thin body, hold it flat, and supply it with water and nutrients while carrying off glucose for storage in the roots. And I realize that this is the same principle—the identical "design"—that insects employ for the construction of their wings. This in turn makes me think of the universality of many laws of nature, of the interrelationship of all natural things—animals, plants, and minerals. And I think of us human beings who, notwithstanding our vaunted civilization, our technology, our sophistication, and our religious beliefs, will perish miserably if we ever lose our contact with nature.

A desert plant held up against the sky reveals the high degree of
structural organization found even in the humblest weed.

Above: Cross-bedded sandstone in Utah. *Opposite*: A piece of broken oyster shell, magnified about twelve times linear. The similarity between the two structures is striking, both having evolved by accretion. The mollusk added layer to layer in growth; the rock gradually was built up by layers of water-deposited or wind-driven sand, which, in the course of eons, solidified into stone.

In each case, minute particles were added to one another over a period of time, here through the action of the living mollusk, there by the forces of water and wind. Growth, normally associated only with the evolvement of living things, has been accomplished. How can we draw a line between what is alive and what is inanimate—the living mollusk, its rocklike limy shell, the stone?

Above: Cross-section of the trunk of an American elm reveals its internal structure—the annual rings of growth. *Opposite*: Cross-section through a nodule of calcium carbonate deposited layer by layer over a period of time. Both structures ''grew'' through accretion—a method shared by minerals, animals, and plants.

Above: A puffball (*Calvatia cyathiformis*), a mushroom. *Opposite*: Snakeskin chert, a mineral. Both are examples of the division of a surface into sections caused by surface tension.

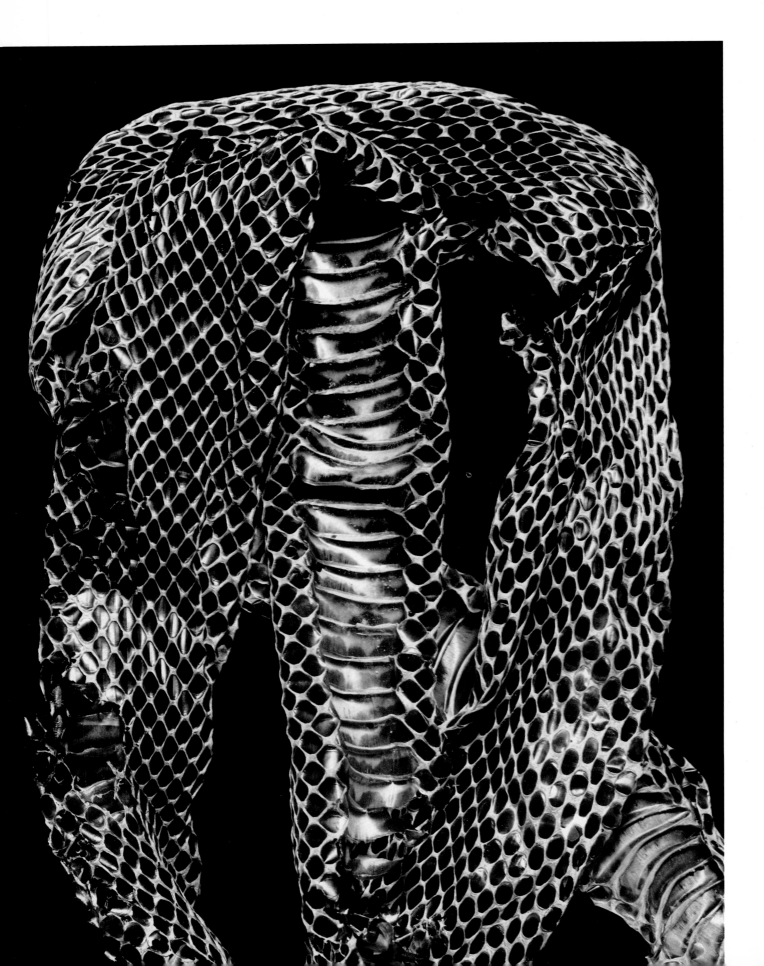

Scales and scalelike arrangements (see the following spread) are structural devices used by animals as well as plants. *Above:* Exquisitely tapered toward both the front and the rear of the fish's body, these scales rival in precision of execution the best mechanical creations, a joy to behold, an embodiment of sheer beauty. *Opposite:* The shed skin of a blacksnake, cellophane-thin, diaphanous, still holds its scaly design.

Above: A close-up of the enormous leaf stalks of a Traveler's Tree (*Ravenala madagascariensis*), which form its trunk. *Opposite*: Shoot of a succulent plant. In both cases, the overlapping arrangement of leaves resembles scales.

Above: Crystals of black quartz. The quintessence of hardness and precision. *Opposite*: A dendrite. Dendrites (from the Greek word *dendron*, meaning tree) are not petrified plants, but the remainder of mineralized solutions that infiltrated cracks in rocks, spread along the fracture planes, and crystallized as they dried. Their manner of growth is fascinating because of its uncanny similarity to that of plants: a stem or trunk dividing successively into smaller and smaller branches, which amazingly never cross one another or even touch. Why this is so is not known.

Above: Queen Anne's lace. *Opposite*: Cow parsnip. Constructed according to the principle of radial symmetry (see p. 115), these plants are marvels of structural engineering, achieving maximum efficiency with minimum use of building material to accomplish their purpose: to expose their blossoms to pollinating insects.

Above: The fibrous skeleton of a sea cucumber. *Opposite*: The woody skeleton of a cholla cactus. Both structures utilize the principle of the space frame in tubular form to achieve maximum strength with minimum material and weight. Designs such as these could arouse envious admiration—and respect— in any human engineer.

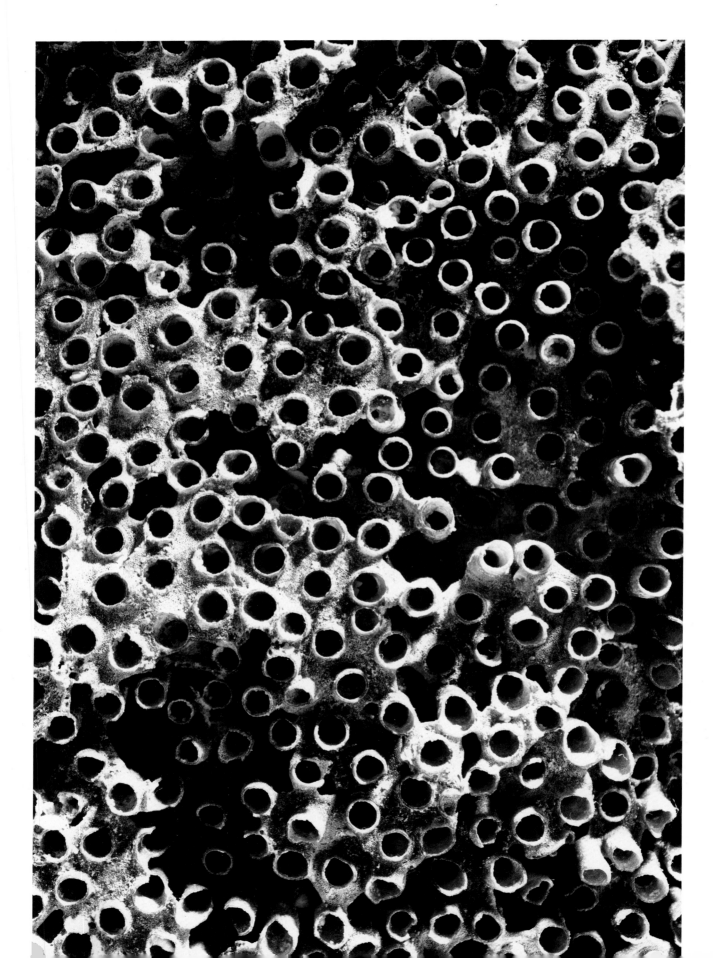

Coral—the hard, calcareous skeleton secreted by certain anthozoans. The tubular constructions of this particular species resemble the kind of boiler used in old-fashioned locomotives and modern power plants. As always in nature, maximum efficiency is achieved with minimum use of construction material. The left picture shows the tubes in which the tiny animals live head-on; the right one is in side-view to expose the internal bracing.

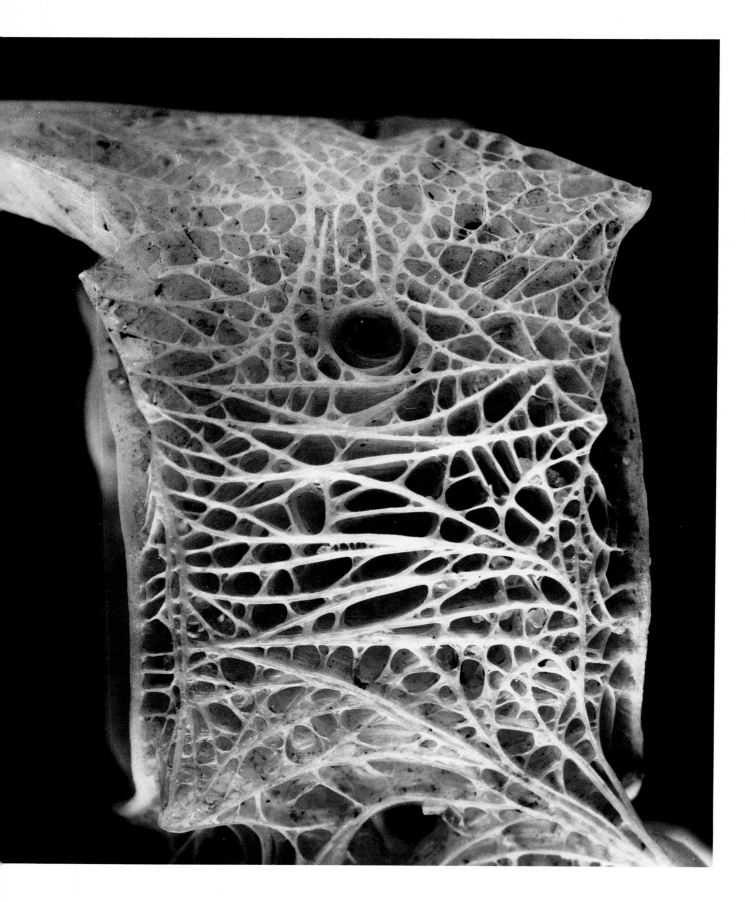

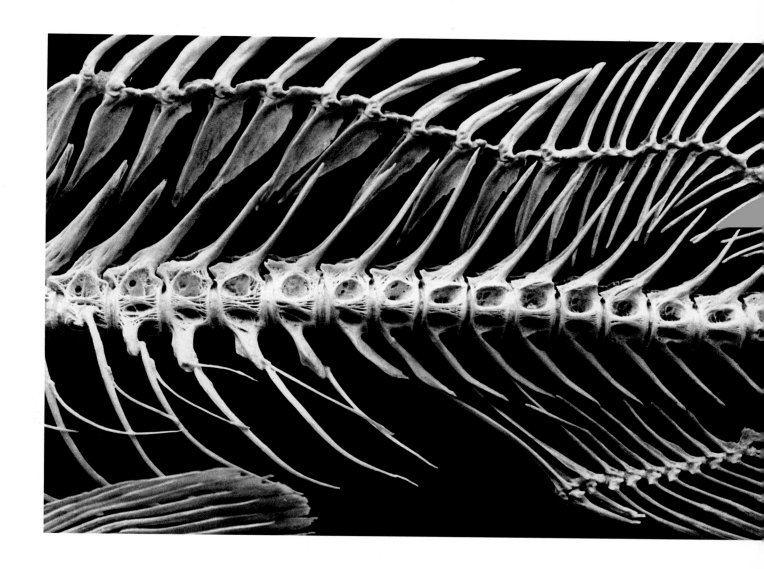

As a former architect and structural engineer, I have always been fascinated by bones. Some, such as the fish vertebra shown on the opposite page, are three-dimensional stress diagrams, which make me see and feel the forces they have to withstand. Others, such as the skeleton of a fish (*above*), are admirable for their exquisite execution, precision, and beauty. To handle clean, dry bones, to touch their forms, their smoothness, their curves, can be a delightful, sensuous experience.

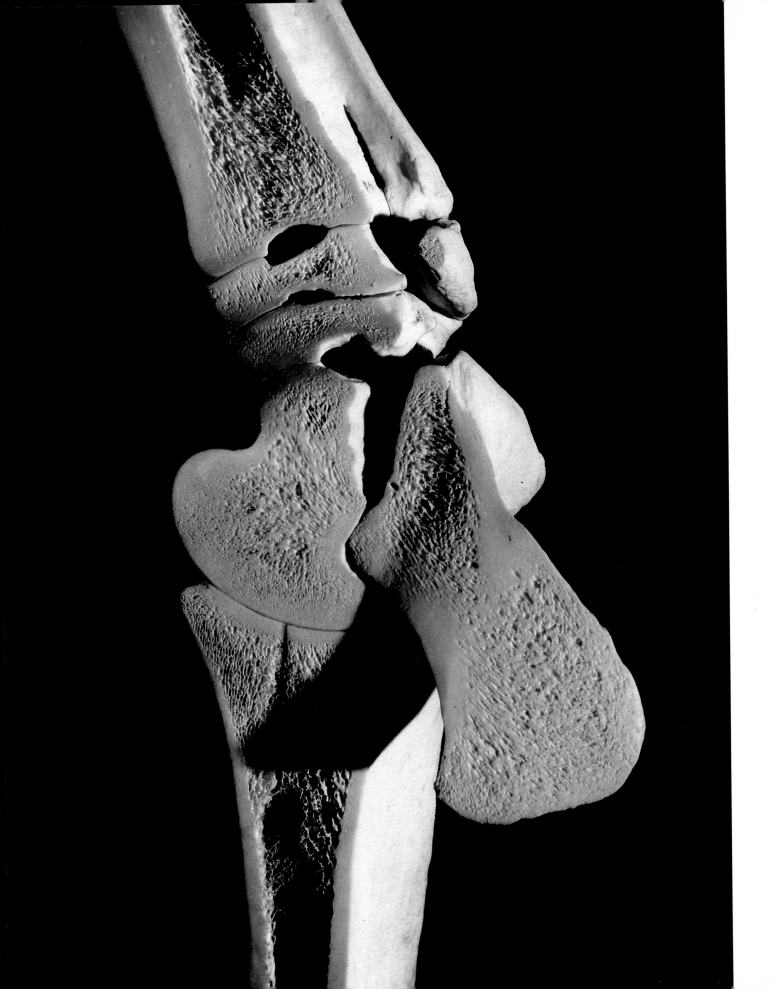

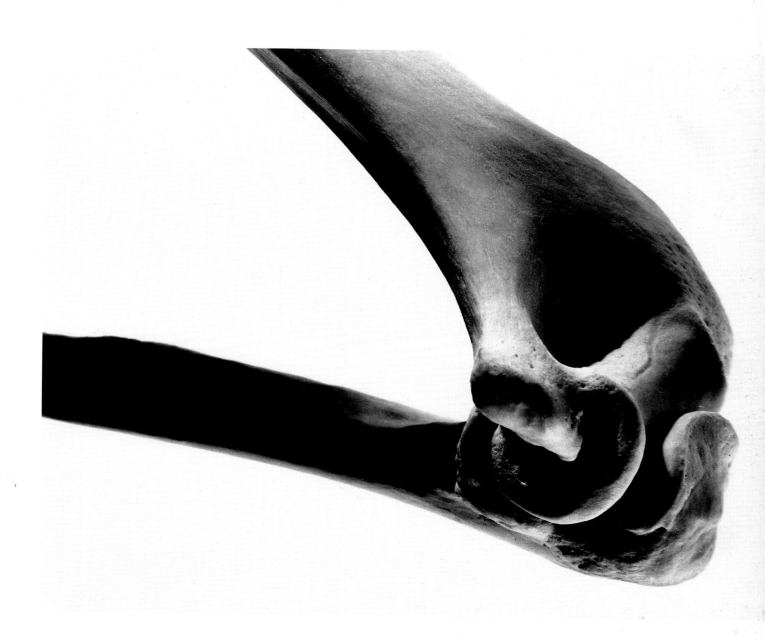

Skeletal articulation in vertebrates is mainly based upon the principle of rotary motion: most of the bones are joined in such a way that movement is essentially circular, the bone rotating about a stationary hinge or ball-and-socket joint. More complicated movements of limbs—as in hands, feet, or wings—are produced through a combination of rotary motions by several joints. *Above*: The hingelike human elbow joint. *Opposite*: Two views of the heel assemblage of a horse show the same structure in two different sections, one rotated 90 degrees relative to the other.

The variety and ingenuity of structures belonging to the plant kingdom stagger the imagination. Shown here are two extremes: tumbleweed (*above*) and the flower- and seed-bearing stems of a grass (*opposite*). The first is designed to roll and tumble with the prairie wind to distribute its seeds. The second stands tall with stems, whose ratio between diameter and height exceeds that of any man-made structure.

Leaves are the factories that directly or indirectly produce out of inorganic material the food for everything alive. The principle of their construction is as simple as it is effective: a membrane stiffened by a framework of veins. This basic principle, however, can take almost any conceivable form. *Opposite*: The complete system of veins of a leaf whose soft substance has been removed by chemical means. *Above*: A fallen elm leaf displays its supporting veins.

Leaves produce food by photosynthesis, a process powered by light. To produce most efficiently, leaves are always arranged in such a way that each receives maximum light or that they shade each other as little as possible. The resulting growth pattern, which always is characteristic of the respective species of plant or tree, is called a *leaf mosaic*. Shown here are a sugar maple seedling seen on axis (*above*) and the tip of a branch from a black birch (*opposite*). In each case, the regular, symmetrical, "shadowless" arrangement guarantees maximum light for each leaf.

White mulberry. Leaf mosaics collected from two different trees. Overlapping of leaves is virtually avoided.

Leaves and feathers are constructed according to the same principle:
a midrib from which branches extend in two opposite directions.
Above: An asparagus leaf. *Opposite*: A feather. The resemblance is
striking.

Although the construction principle of all feathers is the same, when needed, this principle can be varied to an almost infinite degree. But no matter what its size, color, texture, or design, each feather is a masterpiece in its own right.

IV. Variations on a Theme

Nature's designs are infinite. Yet it soon becomes apparent that many of these at first so different appearing patterns are actually only variations of a relatively small number of basic designs.

Take, for example, leaves. Among the trillions of leaves in the world, probably no two are exactly alike. Yet upon closer study we find that this astronomical number of different leaves can be classified in only a few basic designs of two main groups: needlelike or scalelike leaves and broad leaves. The broad leaves in turn belong to only two subgroups: simple leaves and compound leaves.

The same principle can be found again and again among the objects of nature. On the following pages I will present two examples: tree bark and teeth.

Bark is the external covering of the woody parts of a tree. Its purpose is to protect. While the principle is simple, its practical execution can take on countless different forms. Each form is characteristic of a specific kind of tree, which evolved according to its particular needs, which in turn were dictated by the environment. As a result, tree bark can range from white to black and from silky-smooth to deeply ridged, patterned in a multitude of different combinations. Each design is so specific for the respective tree that it becomes a personal mark, a clue to identification.

Teeth serve a double purpose: to seize and chew food and for defense. As with leaves and bark, the form that teeth take varies enormously according to the needs of their owners; yet each design, no matter how bizarre, is still only a variation of the same basic theme.

In this connection, it is interesting to note that teeth as a means of defense have proven so successful in the struggle for life that one of their typical forms, the daggerlike, pointed shape of canine teeth, has become the model for an entire class of defensive structures: spines and thorns—structures not exclusive to animals (porcupines, hedgehogs, spiny anteaters, certain species of lizard and fish) but used also by plants (roses, hawthorns, cacti, and many others). This pattern proves again that the basic laws and forms of nature are relatively few, while their manifestations can vary almost infinitely.

Above: Leaves from a variety of annuals, which I collected near my home. Although the underlying principle is the same in all cases, the differences in execution are remarkable. Also remarkable is that each design is beautiful.
Following pages: Leaves from 11 kinds of woody plants. They are from left to right and top to bottom on the left-hand page: black oak, tulip tree, American bittersweet, tulip tree, and fox grape. On the right-hand page: slippery elm, sugar maple, red oak, white oak, American basswood, and red maple. Each leaf's design is so characteristic of its respective species that it can be used for identification. (See diagram below.)

1. Black oak
2. Tulip tree
3. American bittersweet
4. Tulip tree
5. Fox grape
6. Slippery elm
7. Sugar maple
8. Red oak
9. White oak
10. American basswood
11. Red maple

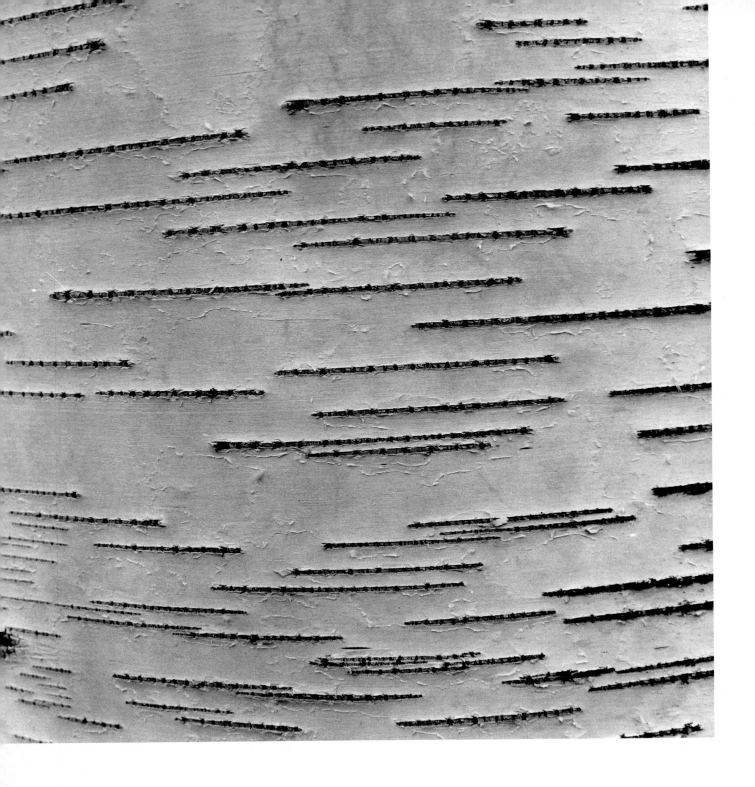

Although the purpose of any kind of bark is to protect the woody parts of a tree, this goal can be achieved in many different ways. Shown on this and the following four spreads are 10 different bark designs, each so typical for its respective species that, like a leaf, it can serve as an aid in identification. Shown above is the bark of gray birch, on the opposite page that of sycamore or plane tree.

Bark of paper birch.

Bark of shagbark hickory.

Bark of locust tree.

Bark of American beech.

As in the cases of leaves and bark, the purpose of teeth is basically the same. However, since the specific requirements of different kinds of animals vary according to their needs, teeth can vary enormously in their design. Examples of rather unusual teeth are the tusks (actually canine teeth) of a warthog (*above*) and a walrus (*opposite*).

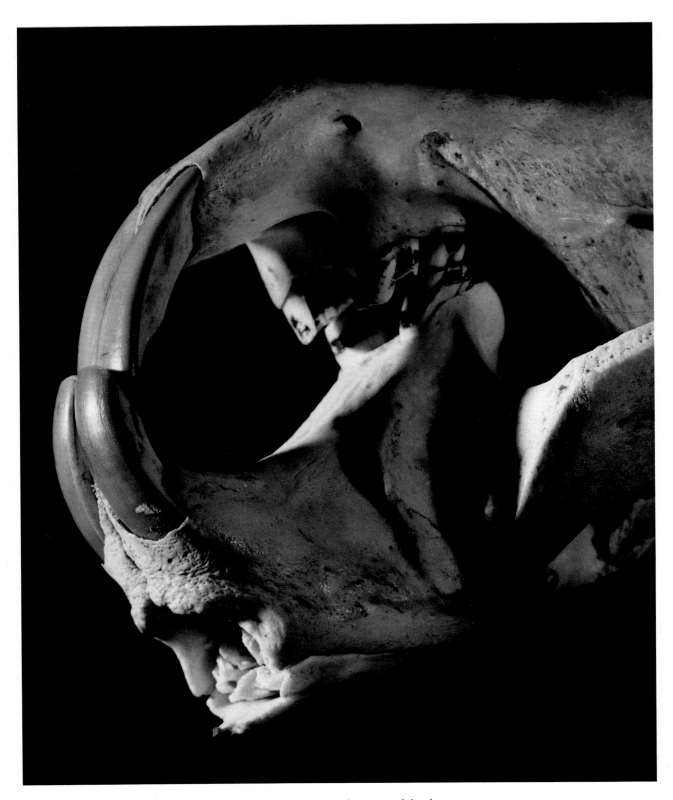

Above: Detail of the skull of a beaver. *Opposite*: Close-up of the front of a lion's skull. The photo above shows the incisors; the second photo shows the canine teeth. In each case, the owner's needs decide which kind of teeth are most prominently developed.

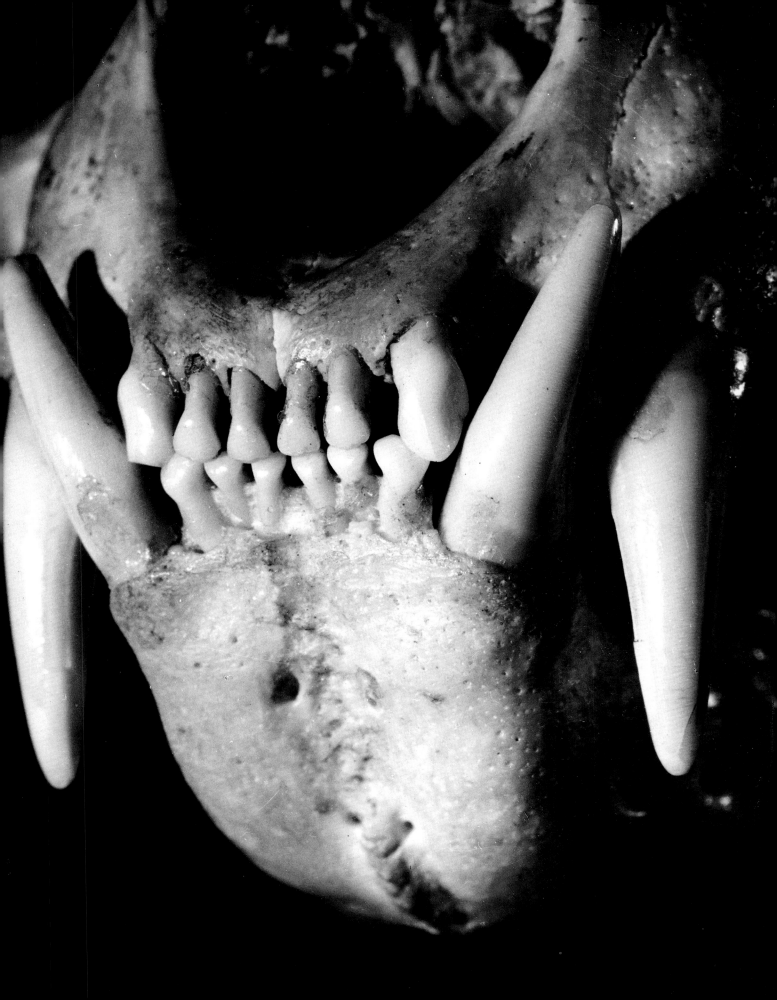

Shown on this spread are two highly specialized types of teeth.
Above: The buzzsaw-like teeth of a skate, a fish related to the rays
and sharks. *Opposite*: The "teeth" of a Venus flytrap leaf (*Dionaea
muscipula*), a carnivorous, insect-eating plant. Its leaves are equipped
with tiny hairs sensitive to touch that act like triggers when activated
by a potential victim, causing the two halves of the leaf to close like
the jaws of a trap. The interlocking "teeth" prevent escape, and
digestive fluids secreted by the plant then make a meal of the intruder.

Above: Blowfish; the thornlike spicules covering its entire body make it most unattractive to predators, fulfilling the function of defensive teeth. *Opposite*: Venus comb shell; in addition to stabilizing the shell on the sea floor, the needle-sharp spines undoubtedly also serve as deterrents to potential enemies.

V. Symmetry

One universal principle ruling the organization of many of nature's structures is symmetry. It manifests itself in two forms: bilateral and radial. Examples of both are shown on the following pages.

Two aspects of symmetry in nature are particularly thought-provoking. First, there is the fact that structures so "sophisticated," so highly organized as to qualify as "symmetrical," seem to grow spontaneously out of inorganic matter—carbon dioxide and water—which provides the basic material for plants and animals. Then there is a puzzling question: among symmetrical structures, how does one side (in the case of bilateral symmetry as in birds or butterflies) or one segment (in the case of radial symmetry as in daisies or starfish) "know" what the other side or the adjacent segment is doing, so that it can mirror it?

Above: An unspecified plant. *Opposite*: Fox grape vine.

Dandelion seed crown. This ephemeral, incredibly delicate, three-dimensional, radial-symmetrical structure is one of the most perfect and beautiful of all of nature's creations.

Marguerite. With its bright yellow petals emanating in radial
symmetry from a central disk, this lovely flower to me is a symbol of
the sun, radiating warmth and happiness.

Examples of radial symmetry in nature. *Above*: Gilled mushrooms.
Opposite: One half of a piece of coral buried in the sand. Again, we
can observe how two totally unrelated forms of life developed
structurally along identical lines.

Euphorbia obesa, a radial-symmetrical plant.

Sea urchin, a radial-symmetrical echinoderm.

Above: A starfish. *Opposite*: A sand dollar—a flat, disklike sea urchin.
As in all echinoderms, body organization is radial-symmetrical.

VI. The Spiral

As in symmetry, the spiral is one of nature's basic forms of design. We see it in structures as large as galaxies (above) and as small as snails (opposite page) and DNA molecules.

Geometrically speaking, a spiral results if a point is moved around a fixed point while receding from or approaching it at a uniform rate. This makes spirals more sophisticated structures than the random clumping of inorganic matter, such as the molecules and chemical components that form all rocks, plants, and animals.

The most beautiful and geometrically perfect spirals are found in the shells of the chambered nautilus (page 130) and some other sea shells (sundial shell, miraculous Thatcheria; page 126). Other natural spirals occur in countless other mollusks (the gastropods), in the growth patterns of many vines, the arrangement of sunflower seeds, the structure of many cacti (page 139), the twisted trunks of certain trees (pages 128–129), and the strands of orb spider webs (page 151).

A particularly fascinating form of spiral organization is found in the arrangement of sunflower seeds, the scales of pine cones, the florets of daisies, the blossoms of Queen Anne's lace, the bumps on pineapples, and the spines of certain cacti. These grow in the form of two sets of spirals, interlocked, one curving clockwise, the other counterclockwise, like opposite directed pinwheels. What is most remarkable and so far unexplained is the fact that the number of spirals in each set nearly always coincides with two adjacent numbers of the Fibonacci series—a fact so fascinating that a special subchapter beginning on page 132 is devoted to it.

Opposite: The spiral galaxy Canes Venatici (NGC 5194–5); courtesy Mt. Wilson and Palomar Observatories. *Above*: A snail—a gastropod, a lump of animated slime—produces a geometrically almost perfect spiral billions of times all over the world on land and in the sea. The next time you see a snail—in your garden, in the woods, on the beach—pick it up, examine it, enjoy its beauty, the perfection of its curves, then let your mind wander along the spiral path from snails to galaxies.

Below: A marine mollusk (*Thatcheria mirabilis* Sowerby); a spiral as sharp and precise as if cut on a lathe. *Opposite*: Tentacles of a grape vine; tough and powerful as coiled steel.

Trunks of evergreens high in the Sierras, stripped in death of their
bark, reveal the spiral growth pattern of the tree.

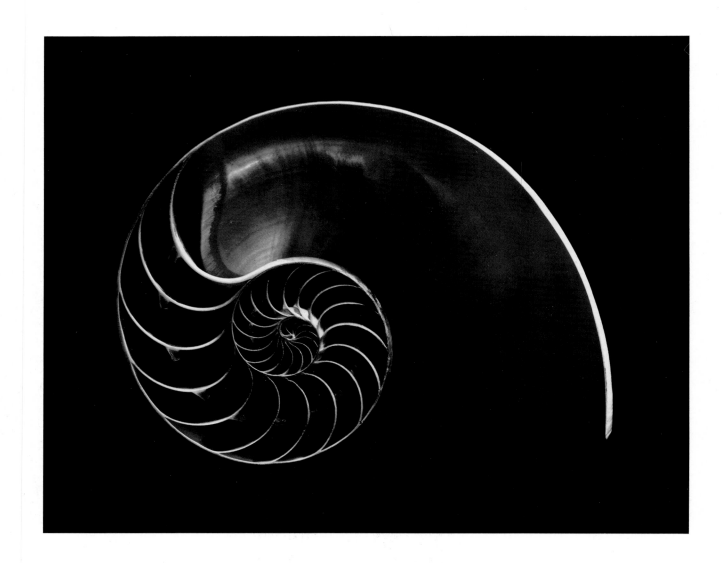

Sectioned shell of a chambered nautilus, displaying an almost mathematically precise equiangular or logarithmic spiral: if radii were drawn from the shell's center, they would intersect the spiral at identical angles.

A common millipede (class *Diplopoda*) coiled in defensive position. Seeing this spiral in all its perfection I wonder why some people express horror at the sight of these harmless, defenseless animals, which neither bite nor sting and are not ''slimy'' but hornlike and dry to the touch.

A FASCINATING "COINCIDENCE"

One of the most intriguing aspects of design in nature is the relationship between the Golden Section, the Fibonacci numbers, and the growth pattern of certain plants. Here are the facts:

Act 1. The most famous of all beauty canons is the Golden Section, which establishes the most aesthetically appealing ratio between the two sections of a line divided into two unequal parts or the two dimensions of a rectangle. It can be expressed by the equation $a:b = b:(a + b)$ in which a represents the smaller and b the larger of the two entities involved. In graphic form, it looks like this:

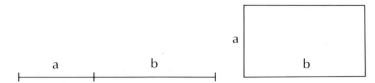

Numerically expressed, if we assume that a has a value of 1, the corresponding value of b would be 1.6180355. This ratio can be expressed as follows: $1:1.6180355 = 0.6180334$. Note the last number; in a little while, it will crop up in an unexpected place.

Act 2. The Fibonacci numbers. This is an unending sequence in which each number represents the sum of its two predecessors:

$$1, 1, 2, 3, 5, 8, 13, 21, 34, 55, 89, 144, 233, 377, \text{etc.}$$

If we write any two adjacent numbers of this sequence in the form of a ratio, we will find a most surprising similarity to the ratio expressed in the Golden Section and the number 0.6180334. For example:

2:3 = 0.6666666	0.0486332
3:5 = 0.6000000	0.0180334
5:8 = 0.6250000	0.0079666
8:13 = 0.6153846	0.0026488
13:21 = 0.6190475	0.0010141
21:34 = 0.6176470	0.0003864
34:55 = 0.6181818	0.0001484
55:89 = 0.6179775	0.0000559
89:144 = 0.6180555	0.0000221
144:233 = 0.6180257	0.0000077
233:377 = 0.6180371	0.0000037

The right-hand column is the one I find particularly interesting; it shows the *difference* between the value of a specific Fibonacci ratio (for example, 2:3 = 0.6666666) and the value of the ratio of the Golden Section (0.6180334). Comparing these differences we find that they get smaller as the value of the Fibonacci numbers increases. In other words, a direct relationship exists between paired numbers of the Fibonacci sequence and the ratio of the Golden Section: the higher the value of a pair of Fibonacci numbers, the more closely their ratio approaches that of the Golden Section until eventually the two become identical.

Act 3. Specific components of certain plants grow in the form of two sets of spirals curving clockwise and counterclockwise, respectively, like opposite directed pinwheels. Examples are the seeds of sunflowers, the florets of daisies, the bumps on pineapples, the scales of pine cones, the thorns of certain cacti, and so on. What makes this form of arrangement not only aesthetically pleasing but thought-provoking is that each species always has its own number of spirals and that the number of spirals in each set invariably coincides with two adjacent numbers of the Fibonacci sequence. In sequoia cones, for example, the number of spirals is 3 and 5, in pine cones 5 and 8, in pineapples and some cacti 8 and 13, in other cacti 13 and 21, in most daisies 21 and 34, and in most sunflowers 55 and 89.

Finale. I know of no explanation for this remarkable relationship between the Golden Section and the Fibonacci sequence on one hand, and certain aspects of plant design on the other. To call it "coincidence" seems to me avoiding the issue—the agreement is too perfect for that. An underlying law of nature must be involved—a law still to be defined. No matter what the explanation and whether it will ever be found, that a connection exists among three apparently unrelated phenomena is undeniable. At present it is a mystery. But then, I find *genuine* mysteries thought-provoking—proof that we still have much to learn, perhaps that there is more in this world and to life than we will ever know.

Above: Sequoia cones; the spiral arrangement of their knobs is 3 and 5—three spirals going one way, five the other. *Opposite*: Florets of a daisy; the spiral arrangement of most daisies is 21 and 34.

Here is another interesting item: I recently found a cactus (shown on p. 139) whose spines were arranged in two opposing sets of 17 and 28 spirals, respectively—numbers that don't occur in the Fibonacci series. The interesting fact is this: if, for some reason, the number of spirals in one set had to be 28, the number of spirals in the other set resulting in a ratio that comes closest to that of the Golden Section is 17 (17:28 = 0.6071428, which is closer to the Golden Section equivalent of 0.6180334 than either the ratio 18:28 = 0.6428571 or the ratio 16:28 = 0.5714285).

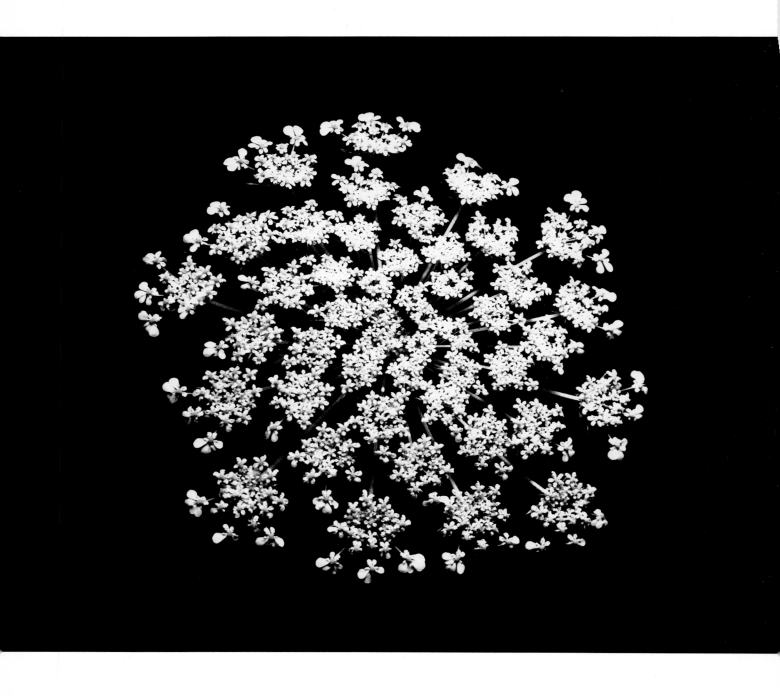

Above and *opposite*: Queen Anne's lace. I see a swirling spiral galaxy in the photograph above, a design of cosmic implications. On the opposite page, the picture of a similar flower after it has finished blooming shows even more clearly the pattern of opposing spirals typical of these plants, a pattern which, outdoors in nature, is not always easy to recognize.

Pine cone. The number of opposing spirals is 8 and 13.

Cactus (see comments on p. 134). The number of spirals is 17 and 28.

VII. Animal Constructs

As mentioned before, for the purpose of this book, nature's designs are classified in one of two categories: planned (the forms of living things) and fortuitous (the forms of erosion). The first class can break into two subgroups: (1) planned by nature and executed in accordance with instructions encoded in the genes, and (2) planned by animals and executed by them in accordance with their instinctive drives. To the latter category belongs everything made by animals, from beaver dams and bird nests to spiderwebs. These are the animal constructs.

Two things make animal constructs particularly interesting to me: the ingenuity and skill with which these objects are made, and the fact that generally these gifts are inborn and neither taught by the parents nor learned by observing other animals of the same species. They are part of the creature's genetic heritage. These animals simply "know."

How astonishing and miraculous this is becomes clear the moment we take a closer look at these constructs and think about the selection of the building material (as in the case of beaver dams, bird nests, or hornet nests), selection of the building site, and planning and executing the work itself. Look, for example, at an orb spider's web. The web's diameter is often 20 or 30 times the size of its builder, and it is attached to the tips of twigs difficult to reach. Yet its complex geometrical design is all in one plane—the web is flat. How did the spider "visualize" the final result in order to "plan" it and lay it out correctly? How did it know where to attach the main stays, how to measure the the distance between the radial strands, how to construct the spiral? And all this in darkness; spider webs are nearly always built at night.

A similar miracle occurs in the building of a hornet nest or an ant hill, whose architectural concepts rival, and in certain aspects surpass, many comparable human designs. And in these cases the structure is not the work of a single animal, but the result of coordinated group activity by hundreds or thousands of individual insects involving intercommunication. Ants or hornets in effect "talk" to each other and agree on a complex design! "Anthropomorphic and unscientific," you may think—but what other explanations are there? There is no doubt that these insects work in concert, which presupposes communication of some kind, whether by sound ("words"), smell, touch, gestures, or thought transference. Look at the inside of a hornet nest (pages 144–145) and marvel. . . .

Opposite: Nest of ruby-throated hummingbird. Many hummingbirds stick bits of moss and lichen, vegetable down, and pieces of spiderweb to the outside of their nests for camouflage. As a result these nests are virtually invisible, appearing to be irregularities in the growth of the supporting tree.

Nest of red-eyed vireo. The skill with which these tiny birds can
combine pine needles, blades of dry grass, twigs, and other nonsticky
objects and mold them into a coherent structure is uncanny,
especially if one considers that no parent taught the builders the
basics of nest construction; this knowledge is instinctive, inherited.

A colony of cliff swallows have built their potterylike nests in the
shelter of an overhanging bluff in Utah. Each nest is constructed of a
large number of individual pellets of mud and forms a thin-walled
shell, as can be seen in this picture. These are the same birds as the
famous swallows of the Mission of San Juan Capistrano in California.

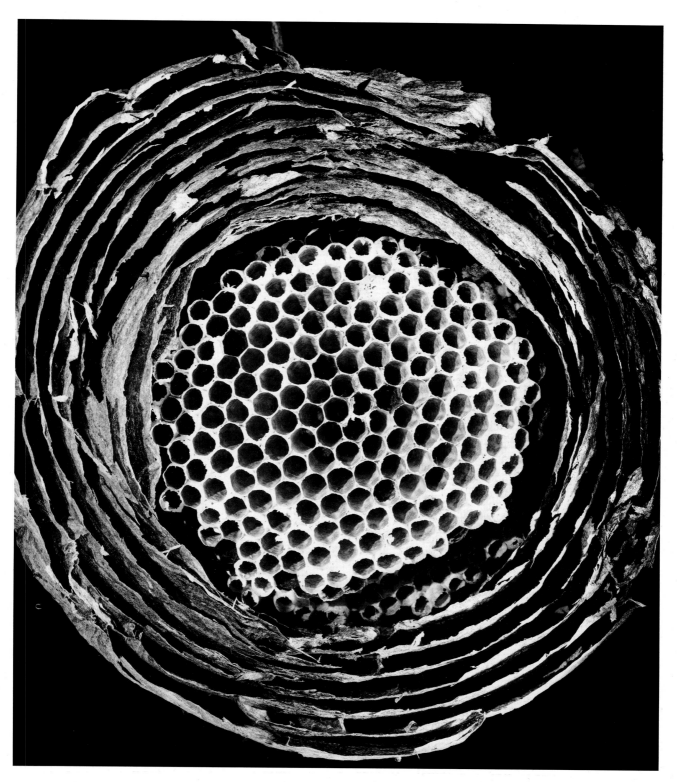

Two views of the inside of the nest of the bald-faced hornet (*Vespula maculata*) showing the tiers of horizontal combs (*opposite*), the packaging of the cells (*above*), and a cross-section of the encasing wall. This wall consists of layers of a paperlike substance separated by air spaces for equally effective insulation against heat and cold. Scientific measurements have established that the insulating power of this structure, which was only one and three-quarters inches thick, is equivalent to that of a 16-inch thick brick wall. Whereas one cubic inch of brick masonry weighs 27.1 grams, the equivalent volume of this hornet nest wall material weighs only 0.2 grams.

Egg sack of the garden spider (*Argiope aurantia*). Each sack is about the size of a 50 cent piece and contains from 100 to 200 eggs. Strands of silky guy wires form an elastic suspension system that protects the eggs from rough jolts when the supporting weed or branch is buffeted by wind. Human engineers could not have invented a more effective design.

The protective casing of a ''bagworm''—the collective popular name of the larvae of the moth family *Psychidae*. Each species builds its own characteristic ''home'' from bits of twigs and leaves cemented to the outside of an inner sleeve spun of silk in which the caterpillar spends its entire life until transformed into the adult moth.

Orb weaver webs decorating the ironwork of a bridge in Connecticut. The web shown above is unfinished, probably because some mishap befell the spider before it could complete its work—the sticky, insect-trapping spiral is always put in last. Both photographs were made shortly after sunrise before the dew had time to evaporate. Later, when dry, these webs are virtually invisible because their threads are so fine.

Above: The tentlike web of a grass spider (*Agelenopsis*). On cool mornings in fall, large numbers of these sheet webs can often be seen decorating the lawns of New England, where they look like so many silk handkerchiefs spread out to dry. But as soon as the dew, which made them visible, has evaporated they seem to disappear as mysteriously as they came. This picture clearly shows how skillfully these spiders suspend their silken sheets from individual blades of grass, making these structures look like miniature circus tents. *Opposite*: Web of the banded garden spider (*Argiope trifasciata*). At its center, the weaver herself sits waiting for the web to dry so that the daily business of catching insects can begin. Like all orb weavers, she sits with her head facing down, presumably so that in an emergency she can instantly drop to the ground at the end of her silken lifeline.

VIII. Sculpture and Ornamentation

While exploring the functional forms of nature and studying them as an architect and structural engineer, I couldn't help being impressed time and again by the intrinsic beauty of most of these creations. Pondered with an open mind, a leaf—any leaf—is beautiful in its outline, form, and detail. The same is true of a clam shell fragment, like the one shown above as an average person might see it, and on the opposite page as the identical fragment appears photographed in a more revealing light and magnified five times. Its internal structure uncovered by erosion, this apparently insignificant piece of a clam shell rivals in sculptural beauty the grace and rhythm of an ancient frieze.

Surprises like this are common for anyone looking at nature's designs with the same unbiased attitude necessary to enjoy abstract art. Questions such as what is it? what does it mean? are immaterial. The point is, do you like it? Does it affect you emotionally? And ultimately, do you find it beautiful?

It is in this sense that I present on the following pages some objects of nature that affected me as powerfully as great works of abstract art.

The sweep and grandeur of this deeply eroded clam shell resembles the capital of an ancient column. This tiny fragment is actually less than two inches across.

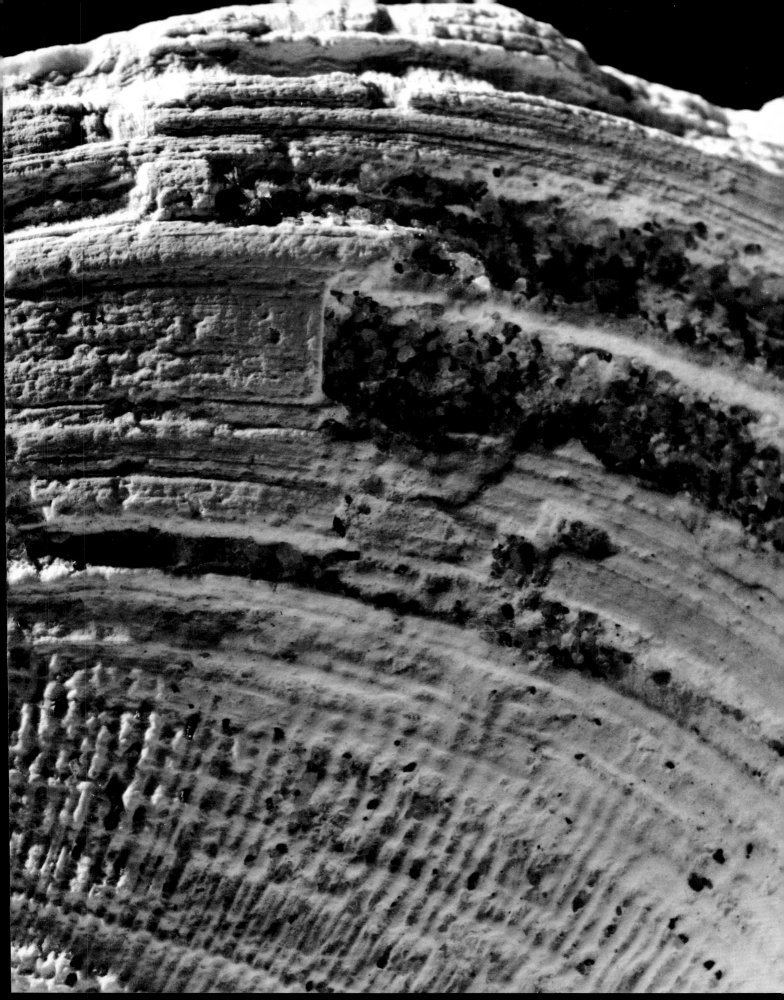

This eroded fragment of a clam shell reminds me of a piece of armor
plate riddled with shell holes, a leftover from a forgotten war.

Seen against the sky, the columella of a whelk assumes the dignity
and power of an ancient column, impressive even in decay.

The pictures on this spread show broken and eroded shells from the Gulf Coast of Florida. They remind me of burned-out strongholds in war, or the portholes of concrete bunkers behind which the guns are waiting.

Seen in the correct perspective and light, broken shells can have the
impact of great abstract sculpture; their effect can be like that of
works by Henry Moore.

I found these shells on Coquina Beach near Bradenton, Florida. I see
in the picture above a statue of Nike, the ancient Greek goddess of
victory, and in the photograph on the opposite page a symbolic
rendition of Death.

Bones are natural sculptures, each bone expressing in three-dimensional form the strains and stresses that it must withstand. Being forms shaped solely by function, bones ipso facto are beautiful. Shown here are two sections of the spines of skates that I found on the beach (*above*), and the fragments of two bird skeletons (*opposite*). These skeletal remains have the same expressive power for me as good abstract sculpture.

Cow vertebrae from the Mojave desert. I see weird creatures in these bones, dancing, cavorting, performing a prehistoric ritualistic ceremony. And on the following spread, these same vertebrae stand silently in monumental loneliness.

Cow vertebrae. Seen in the appropriate perspective, these inch-high bones appear as monumental as the giant stone heads on Easter Island.

Above: Leaves of watermelon peperomia (*Peperomia sanderseei*).
Opposite: Sunflower seeds. Why these leaves and seeds are marked the way they are is not known. Knowledge, however, is not a prerequisite for enjoyment, and so here and on the following two spreads I present examples of beautiful ornamentation in nature.

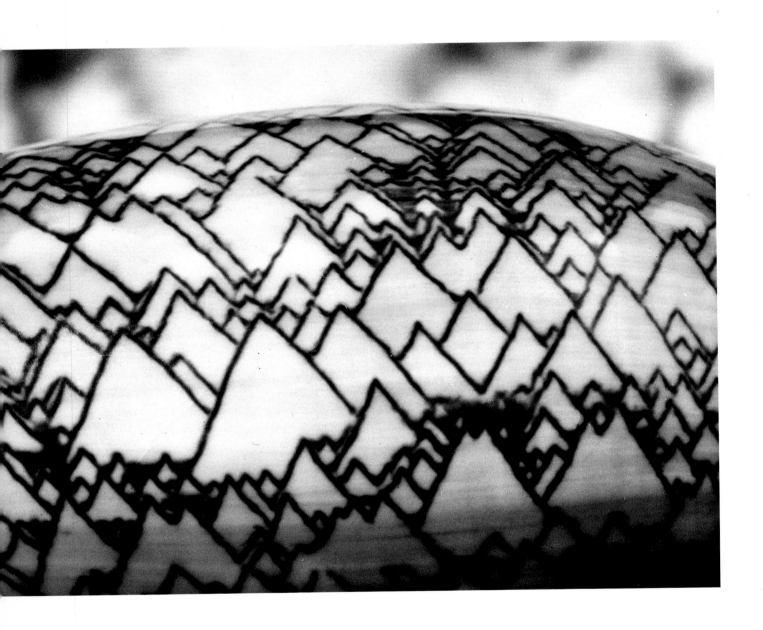

Shell ornamentation. *Above*: Tent olive (*Oliva porphyria*). *Opposite*:
White-banded bubble (*Hydatina albocincta*). What we call
"ornamentation" in nature is actually often camouflage—a device to
make its bearer less conspicuous. Perhaps the purpose of the linear
designs shown here is to visually break up the forms of these shells so
that they don't look like "shells" to predators. But to us, the result is
beauty.

What I said about ornamentation in connection with shells is valid also for birds. Shown here are feather designs of two exotic pheasants. In this case, however, beauty may play a larger role than camouflage since we know that the females of many bird species are attracted by the colors and patterns of the males.